"...babies of course are not human - they are animals, and have a very ancient and ramified culture, as cats have, and fishes, and even snakes: the same in kind as these, but much more complicated and vivid, since babies are, after all, one of the most developed species of the lower vertebrates.

In short, babies have minds which work in terms and categories of their own which cannot be translated into the terms and categories of the human mind.

It is true they look human - but not so human, to be quite fair, as many monkeys."

—Richard Hughes, <u>A High Wind In Jamaica</u>

SORT OF BOOKS

presents

THE BOOK OF
LEVIATHAN

by Peter Blegvad

By the seat of our pants ad astra.

The Book of Leviathan

for Chloë, Kaye and Viggo

Thanks to Mark Ellingham, Natania Jansz, Rafi Zabor, Julian Rothenstein, Edwin Belchamber, Tim Chester, John Paige, amd Simon Lucas. Also to Richard Williams, Liz Jobey, Ian Jack, Nikki Moore, Ruth Metzstein, Henry Porter, et al (especially in scanning) at the *Independent on Sunday Review*, 1991-1999

Published in 2000 by Sort Of Books
PO Box 18678, London NW3 2FL

Distributed by the Penguin Group in all territories excluding the United States and Canada: Penguin Books, 27 Wrights Lane, London W8 5TZ

Printed in Hong Kong by South Sea International Press

160pp
A catalogue record for this book is available from the British Library
ISBN 0-9535227-2-5

"OUR DOLLS DON'T LIVE THROUGH US, WE LIVE THROUGH OUR DOLLS." — WALTER BENJAMIN

TABLE of CONTENTS

I — Lost & Foundling
You're right. He's left. They're gone.

II — Milk
Innocence, in a sense, incenses censors.

III — Dep
From um to Om.

IV — Surely You Jest
A man-size tissue of lies.

V — Terra Incognita
The world as we know it.

VI — Schema Things
The beaten track hits back.

VII — Nameless Dread
Trepidation is a trip.

VIII — Words Enough & Time
Tempus fuggit.

IX — Wilds, Woods & Gas
101 Damnations

X — I Got a Million of 'em
An oasis of sanity in a world GONE MAD.

XI — Hell
Come on down!

XII — Escape
There's one bored every minute.

XIII — Tell Me a Story
Beginning, muddle & end.

XIV — Songs
In which things too foolish to be said are sung.

XV — This Way Up
To be taken lying down.

XVI — A Problem Aired
To air is human.

XVII — The Truck is Stuck
Tale fin.

Introduction
by Rafi Zabor

Q: How did you get the idea of naming a tiny baby Leviathan?

A: From my own kids: they're born, you bring them home and they're bigger than anything else in your life.

Q: Why did you switch from Levi's parents to the Cat?

A: The Cat was easier to draw.

The first time I saw Peter Blegvad's *Leviathan* in *The Independent on Sunday*—and as an American wandering back and forth across the Atlantic in the early nineties, I tended to see it in fragmentary fashion, on visits to France and England—I responded with a spontaneous yelp of pleasure, and within a few encounters with the strip it was clear to me that it was one of the very best things being written, drawn, sung, sculpted, played, danced or acted at the time, an impression the intervening years have done nothing to dim, harumph et cetera. I knew Blegvad's name—it's one you don't easily forget—because about ten years earlier I had reviewed a record, *Kew. Rhone,* he'd been involved with, and he'd sent me a postcard to say thanks for the nice review and to point out that a lyric I had praised as an instance of intelligent surrealism—"Peel's foe, not a set animal, laminates a tone of sleep"—was also a palindrome; but that was it, we'd had no further contact and I had no personal or ulterior motive for going bughouse about his brainchild. I just did. Whenever I was in Europe, spontaneous yelp of pleasure followed spontaneous yelp of pleasure in a tight weekly sequence, nipping at each others' heels, frolicking in the roadside pastures, and assuming looser formations when I could find a copy Stateside or convince a friend to clip an installment and send it over.

It is also true that I have met a few intelligent, literate, artistically sophisticated people who just don't *get* it, and their non-response to what is obviously and just for starters a classic of its kind, assuming it has a kind, has always puzzled me. Maybe they lack an appetite for metaphysical funnies, or are plagued by an allergy to the air of other planets—who knows?—but they're missing out on one of the treats of the present age, and a whole series of bracing violations of the stale prosy treaties of quotidian perception.

This collection tilts away from the metaphysical intricacies of some of Leviathan's darker passages—although in fact it opens with one of the eeriest of these—and treats the reader to a purer oxygen of comedy. The first couple of sections anchor the strip in relatively terrestrial and psychological reality—childhood cognition and miscognition, makeshift household cosmologies, parental incomprehension, sibling rivalry—the better to support the unearthly oddities to come when—Cat replacing Parents and a cosmic puzzlement overwhelming the family dynamic—*Leviathan* decants us into a world not so much fallen as tipped over: realms of dimensional slippage, cognitive puns, and mirrored halls of infinite paradox and *double-comprendre*. It is strange but finally not unfamiliar country.

Installments that continue to leave me fairly helpless with laughter even after many viewings include the conjunction of a heavily armored robot and a Hamlin Garland poem, the appearance of a frothing ectoplasmic Hegel to explain "the opposite of bunny", the ludicrously funny Bark Ode panel (in which, *sotto voce*, that hymning, lyring dog and his rapt audience index an elemental feel for the vanity, poignancy and limits of life in any species: the strip in general sounds a persistent note whose music might humble human supposition), the flawless tautological humor of Leviathan and the locomotive (though note that most people, had they come up with the gag, wouldn't have written the Cat's line, which perfects it), and many, many more. Blegvad's expansive gift for concision may be most evident in the one-panel episode concerning the cut of the other guy's jib (notice also: those boats are round: the sense of detail just doesn't quit). He also seems to own precise access to preconscious memory, of which the alchemical formula for milk may be the most acute example. None of this resembles anything I've seen or read anywhere else, ever.

The drawing ranges from the defiantly home-made to the surprisingly beautiful. It is always apt, and sometimes it can be the key to a subtle door. "Cat's New Look," introduced in the first panel of the sequence in which Leviathan visits Hell, seems a good example. Deciding to draw the Cat differently one week first struck me as an instance of the freedom and simplicity of motion only first-rate talents can manage, that and an unwillingness to be hobgobbled by smallminded consistencies. After a while it emerged as not just a clever-clever demonstration of authorial smarts but as a subtle injunction to remain unruffled, in life as in more quickly passing comix, by the unexpected lurch of secondary elements—all appearances in the strip are subject to unexplained mutation—the better perhaps to pursue a sustaining central essence beyond the noise of change. Blegvad keeps burying the bone deeper and inviting us behind the stage-set and the changing-rooms with their stash of costumes, masks and mirrors to what might actually endure but eludes being nailed in place with a name. (As for the altered Cat, note that in order to make so apparently arbitrary a move and allow it due meaning you need to have invented a master narrative, characters and world that can take such flux without snapping.)

Leviathan does sometimes set an epistemological terror whickering beneath the skin of things, since for all its comedy and obliquity the strip engages straight the strangeness, peril and beauty of finding oneself alive—is this what puts off the odd unreceptive sophisticado? I really couldn't say. I seldom read it without being rewarded by a dose of liberating light, a freshening of perception, and a reanimation of the normal sluggard crawl and stumble of the working brain: Blegvad's baby leaves fresh script incised upon the mind.

But—aside from the obvious fact that we're all faceless babies wandering through a shifting, barely scrutable world with only a cat for tutelary spirit—like what's it all mean, man? As the Lord rhetorically inquired in another publication, "Canst thou draw out Leviathan with an hook?" The answer, I think, is a resounding *nyet*. The Fudd of intellect will never capture the Wabbit of true vision. Words fail. Times change. Cats meow. Leviathan swims in its native deep, glistening through serial sea-green layers, sending off spectra of intelligible light as it steers with ribbed and radiant fins. Whut? It is the finest gnostic comic strip to come out of Britain since the heyday of William Blake, and it's a treat to have this book available. Invite it home. Share it with family and friends. Spend the money. It will make us all a little happier, and welcome a classic into our midst.

Rafi Zabor is the author of *The Bear Comes Home*

I. LOST & FOUNDLING

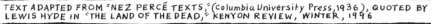
TEXT ADAPTED FROM "NEZ PERCÉ TEXTS," (Columbia University Press, 1936), QUOTED BY LEWIS HYDE IN "THE LAND OF THE DEAD," KENYON REVIEW, WINTER, 1996

(SECOND OF 8 PARTS)

SEVENTH OF 8 PARTS

II. MILK

LEVIATHAN
by PETER BLEGVAD

"a suit of clothes, like a body, spotted with food & shameful behaviour, ..." Yolodia Teitelboim, _Neruda_

UNITED COLOURS OF LEVIATHAN

LEVIATHAN
by Peter Blegvad

My big sister can't sleep without a nightlight. She's afraid of what she calls the "dark".

Ha! Even in the dead of night, this is NOTHING compared to darknesses I've known. Just as Eskimos discern ↗

dozens of gradations of "white" in a vista of ice & snow, ...

- Shark White
- Opal White
- White Cascade
- Hint-O-Shadow
- Mayonnaise
- Ivorine
- Swansdown
- Avalanche

...so I recall different darknesses from my recent past:

1. The darkness which preceded my conception, ...

↳ ARTIST'S IMPRESSION (from UNAIDED MEMORY)

... now THAT was dark!

2. The same darkness, many aeons later, ...

...lit by a twinkle in my father's eye.

3. The Stygian depths I navigated as a spermatozoon.

4. The darkness in which I made myself, cell by cell, following instructions in my mother's blood. I was born with darkness IN MY BONES! I admit, this INNER DARKNESS...

...catches me off-guard sometimes. But I can handle it. INNER DARKNESS...

Highest grade tungsten, non-sag wire in the filament, absorbs voltage surges.

...is no match for INNER LIGHT.

LEVIATHAN
by Peter Blegvad

I've begun to grasp the basics of good taste... Less is definitely more.

That rabbit, frinstance - it's an affront! What do the manufacturers take us for?

Why, there's more charm & character in this little fella's <u>paw</u> than in that vulgar pile of plush...

Bathtime

MAMA!

WHEN THE NURSERY IS DESERTED & THE LIGHTS TURNED OUT...

Give him one for me, Harvey!

TOOT TOOT!

Halp!

NEXT DAY...

I think perhaps it's the natural patina of wear & tear that makes this little guy so loveable.

LEVIATHAN
by Peter Blegvad

REAL DUCKS

D

DU

The Duck in the book does not resemble Real Ducks.

RABBIT

The Rabbit in the book is a monster! The product of a sick mind.

The True Artist has a Responsibility to show things as they really are. First, I'll need some materials...

WILDLIFE

This is harder than it looks. Hold that pose, Rabbit! I want to do you justice.

PAPA

What was that crash? LEVI! STOP WHATEVER YOU'RE DOING!

Here come the critics!

OMYGOD! What have you done to your book?

GLOWING WITH PRIDE

I've interpreted my complex response to Rabbit, rather than merely copy his external appearance...

You've covered it in Peanut Butter! It's ruined!

RABBIT

The True Artist should not expect to be understood or appreciated in his own lifetime...

LEVIATHAN
by Peter Blegvad

A noise at the door. The house is being fed.

A light vegetarian repast.

Sedentary, spell-bound, the house somehow subsists on this frugal salad.

Wish you were here!

Some of it is specially flown in from distant climes. Papa disclaims ownership of the rest of the stuff. It's not his. He says it's "mostly Bill's". Who is Bill? Is his house starving?

Our own shows signs of malnutrition.

What this house needs is a coat of binding emulsion rich in minerals & fats. What this house needs is milk.

White as snow! White as my own unblemished record! Let it fill the rooms up to the attic! Let the house grow up big & strong & healthy.

MY ROOM

MILK

The Tear of a Clown

III. DEP

Z.

LEVIATHAN
by Peter Blegvad

Rebecca's exchange-rate mechanism in action: she gets to stay up late, & in exchange... →

...she won't wet the bed.

She's flexible. She'll solemnly undertake to NOT fill the pockets of her parents' clothes with toothpaste...

Get thee behind me, Satan!

...in exchange for either 7 My Little Ponies or 50 bed-time stories, over a 2 month period.

Honest answers to these three puzzlers:...

Who made God? How much IS that doggy in the window? Why do we die?

... will buy 2 "Thank You"s, 1 "Please", & 3 "Excuse Me"s from this canny capitalist who knows that nothing boosts value like scarcity.

She keeps a scrupulous tally of what she owes.

Let's see... I've been brought 53 drinks of water in the middle of the night over the past 7 months. At the current rate of exchange, that means eating my broccoli with apparent gusto the next 6 times it's served!

1 trip to Euro-Disney = sharing her toys with her little brother for a week.

So go on, Levi, PLAY with them!

Doesn't she UNDERSTAND? Playing doesn't just HAPPEN on command. A person has to wait for the INSPIRATION!

During tense negotiations, the terms of another exchange are thrashed out until all parties are satisfied.

Alright Rebecca, if you come down NOW you can keep him!

IV. SURELY YOU JEST

Chable/Tair thanks to Chris McCourt (see page 46)

V. TERRA INCOGNITA

LEVIATHAN
by Peter Blegvad

LEVIATHAN TAKES STOCK BY MAKING A MAP OF THE WORLD *AS HE KNOWS IT* AND IS DISTURBED TO FIND IT IS ALREADY OVERCROWDED.

Based on The Observer's Book of Larger Moths, by R. L. E. Ford, 1958

LEVIATHAN by Peter Blegvad

A VISIT TO THE *SCIENCE MUSEUM*...

LEVI: ANYTHING IN THERE?
CAT: A SAMPLE OF THE *ETHER*.
LEVI: THE *WHA*...?
CAT: *ETHER*. "AN ELEMENT ONCE...

... THOUGHT TO FILL ALL SPACE BEYOND THE SPHERE OF THE MOON & TO CONSTITUTE THE SUBSTANCE OF THE STARS & PLANETS."

THE ETHER

AH!

& THIS ONE?

CONTAINS *CALORIC*, "A 'SUBTLE FLUID' TO WHICH THE PHENOMENA OF HEAT WERE ONCE ATTRIBUTED."

LEVI: THAT'S 'SUBTLE'!

LOOK, LEVI, *DARK MATTER!* SCIENTISTS SAY 90% OF THE UNIVERSE IS MADE OF THIS STUFF!

WHAT *IS* IT?

NEXT!

CAT: THEY DON'T KNOW. IT SAYS HERE: "POSSIBLY A FAMILY OF PARTICLES OF WHICH NO ONE HAS SEEN THE LEAST EVIDENCE IN THE MOST SENSITIVE EXPERIMENTS."

LEVI: THAT'S 'DARK'!

LAST!

THE EMPEROR'S NEW 'CLOTHES'

WHAT HAVE WE HERE?

THE *LAST* WORD IN UNDERSTATED CHIC!

LEVIATHAN
by Peter Blegvad

In this HOT-HOUSE NURSERY SCHOOL the GENIUSES of TOMORROW are being cultivated.

In the weeds, discarded toys - relics of a discredited view of the UNIVERSE as a stable, symmetrical, law-abiding construct.

"The UNIVERSE is as SHAPELESS as a SPIDER or a blob of SPIT."
Georges Bataille

SPIDER
UNIVERSE
SPIT

FRACTAL BALL

INDETERMINATE TOY

Levi learns how to make from a disk and elastic bands, a whimsical "catastrophe machine." It has unstable bilateral symmetry which suddenly snaps to asymmetry.

SNAP!

NON-EUCLYDIAN BLOCKS

Inside the school, children are taught a new "gospel" which their toys are designed to reinforce.

LEVIATHAN
by Peter Blegvad

Ever hear of the cemetery star?

To steer by its light took skills not taught in any celestial navigation course.

We found the sextant twisted into a figure-8 on the poop-deck & the ship herself high & dry in an overgrown bone-yard, Muswell Hill. Minus her crew, of course.

All hands vanished without trace.

Plates of milky fluid in the mess. A dinner abandoned during the soup course.

The ship was the Salambo, 8,000 tons, out of Copenhagen with a cargo of felt hats, bird seed & bicycle pumps.

She'd snapped her chain in the night & come from her mooring in the Thames, miles across London ...

... to rest among the tombs in the long grass, her short-wave picking up Kinks oldies through a storm of static & mini-cab calls.

How did she get there? "She yawed", the old sailors say. [YAW- to deviate from the straight course as through faulty or unsteady steering.] She was steering by the cemetery star.

VI. SCHEMA THINGS

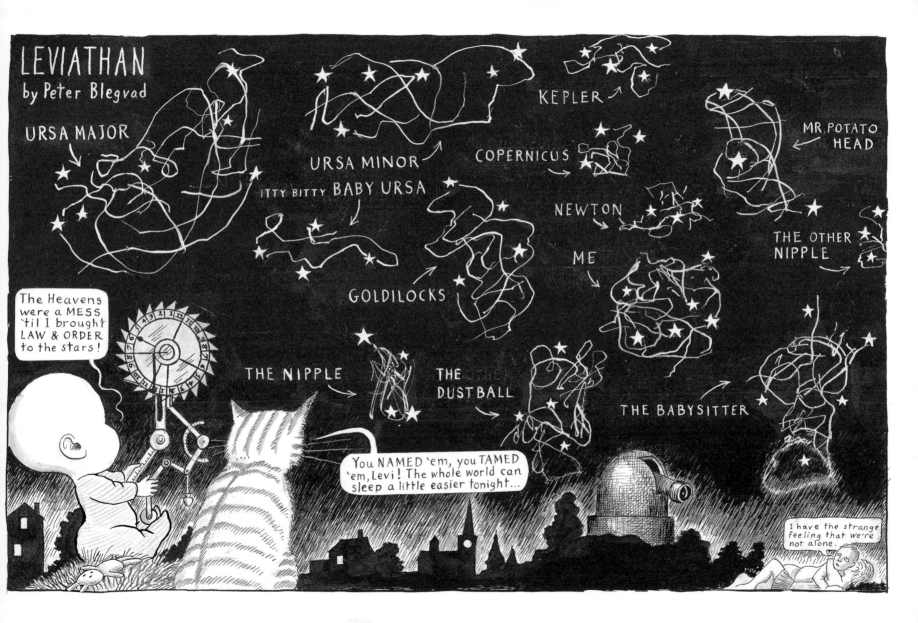

LEVIATHAN
by Peter Blegvad

THE LN 2000 Mk.VI ~ A revolutionary new type of PAPER DART. Marries ancient Origami paper folding with the latest "cut & paste" techniques to produce a BREAKTHROUGH in the PHYSICS of UNPOWERED FLIGHT. An EDUCATIONAL & EXECUTIVE TOY you can make yourself!

STAPLE

FINISHED Mk.VI SHOULD LOOK LIKE THIS. (Strategically placed staple prevents stalling).

(STALLING)

BANZAI!

Mk.VI

FLICK!

Mk.V

Mk.II

Mk.I

Mk.III

Mk.IV

INSTRUCTIONS: 1. CUT ALONG DOTTED LINES. 2. FOLD ALONG SOLID LINES, FOLLOWING NUMBERS. 3. MATCH TABS & GLUE. 4. MICRO-WAVE AT LOW SETTING FOR .03 OF A SECOND OR UNTIL GLUE IS DRY. 5. LAUNCH WITH A FLICK OF THE WRIST, AS SHOWN

LEVIATHAN
by Peter Blegvad

BUS ROUTES

WRINKLES WRULE!

ALL DAY, LEVI "FLEXES" HIS ARM IN ORDER TO STUDY THE INTRICATE WRINKLE SYSTEMS THIS CAUSES IN HIS SLEEVE. HE'S RAPT, READING HIS FORTUNE IN THE FOLDS. IT DOESN'T ESCAPE HIM THAT

WRINKLES "RHYME" WITH OTHER FORMS IN NATURE.

MEANWHILE

OBSERVED

BELIEVE IT OR NOT

IN 1984, WELSH COMPOSER JOHN GREAVES CASUALLY TOSSED HIS JACKET ONTO A CHAIR SO THAT THE WRINKLES FORMED THIS FACE!

ARTIST BURNE HOGARTH, AUTHOR OF "DYNAMIC WRINKLES AND DRAPERY" (Watson-Guptill, 1992), HAS DEFINED THE KINETIC FORCES WHICH GIVE "RISE TO CATEGORICAL SYSTEMS OF WRINKLES AND FOLDS" IN CLOTHING!

ABOVE: Not unlike a research scientist, Hogarth uses diagrams to illustrate his wrinkle theories.

— SWIPED FROM THE COMICS JOURNAL (Fantagraphics)

STONED OUT OF HIS MIND, ALDOUS HUXLEY CLAIMED TO HAVE SEEN "THE ABSOLUTE IN THE FOLDS OF A PAIR OF FLANNEL TROUSERS."

STREUTH!

LEVIATHAN
by Peter Blegvad

L EVI'S BEDROOM, 5:14 A.M.

T HE *BOILER* COMES ON WITH A SOFT *WHOOMPH!*

O UTSIDE, A *TWIG* SNAPS, & A *DOG* BARKS.

D ISTANT DOGS BARK BACK IN *CANINE COLLOQUY.*

A *FOG HORN* SOUNDS IN THE BAY. THOSE THUDS ARE LEVI'S *HEARTBEATS.* THAT HIGH-PITCHED WHINE, HIS *NERVOUS SYSTEM!*

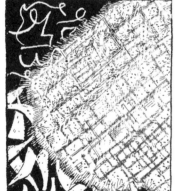

B IRDSONG HERALDS THE DAWN. THE TINTINABULATIONS OF THE *MILKMAN* ARE *ENGULFED* BY A *STREET CLEANING MACHINE.*

A N *ARGUMENT* BREAKS OUT BENEATH LEVI'S WINDOW...

I T GROWS INTO A *BRAWL*— CURSES, SCUFFLING, BLOWS!

A *SHOT* RINGS OUT! NO, IT'S JUST A *CAR* BACKFIRING.

I N THE *CLEAR LIGHT* OF DAY, LEVI'S *SYNESTHESIA* ABATES.

VII. NAMELESS DREAD

VIII. WORDS ENOUGH & TIME

LEVIATHAN
by Peter Blegvad

AUTHOR, JAMES KELMAN, WON THE 1994 BOOKER PRIZE FOR HIS NOVEL, "HOW LATE IT WAS, HOW LATE." IN HIS ACCEPTANCE SPEECH HE SAID:

"IF WE WANT THE BLANK PAGE TO STAY BLANK, THEN LET IT STAY BLANK."
BRAVO! HIS WORDS INSPIRE ME TO PROPOSE A *PRIZE* FOR THE BEST *BLANK PAGE* IN LITERATURE...

THE PRIZE - A BLANK CHEQUE

STILL WITH ME? THEN *LET'S MEET THE CONTESTANTS!*

The Life and Opinions

CHAPTER XVIII

Of Tristram Shandy

CHAPTER XIX

1. THE *SMART MONEY'S* ON THE TWO *BLANK* "CHAPTERS" IN LAURENCE STERNE'S "*TRISTRAM SHANDY*". STERNE SAYS: "I LOOK UPON A CHAPTER WHICH HAS *ONLY NOTHING IN IT* WITH RESPECT; AND CONSIDERING WHAT WORSE THINGS ARE IN THE WORLD..." HE ALSO WISHES THAT "... IT MAY BE A LESSON TO THE WORLD, '*TO LET PEOPLE TELL THEIR STORIES THEIR OWN WAY.*'"

2. "RIDICULOUS!" SCOFFS *ORPHÉE* IN JEAN COCTEAU'S FILM, WHEN SHOWN A COPY OF *NUDISME*, A LITERARY MAGAZINE COMPRISED ENTIRELY OF *BLANK PAGES*...

NUDISME

"IT WOULD BE MORE RIDICULOUS IF IT CONTAINED RIDICULOUS TEXTS." REPLIES HIS COMPANION.

3. PAINTING OF BROTHER BARNABUS "WALKING THROUGH A SNOWSTORM FROM BADEN-BADEN TO CARLSBAD, CLAD IN WHITE PYJAMAS, FOLLOWED BY A FLOCK OF WHITE PONIES. OVERHEAD, AS IF LEADING THE WAY, IS A MYSTIC WHITE GUILLEMOT." FLANN O'BRIEN, *Comhthrom Féinne* III, 1.

4. NO ONE HAS WRITTEN *ABOUT* THE BLANK PAGE WITH MORE PASSIONATE DEVOTION THAN STÉPHANE MALLARMÉ. ACCORDING TO CHARLES MAURON: "WHITENESS, SILENCE, EMPTINESS... OF THE 'VIRGIN PAPER'... ARE TRANSFORMED TO THE HIGHEST IDEAL."

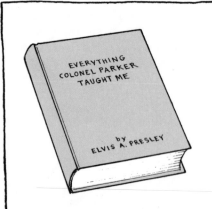

EVERYTHING COLONEL PARKER TAUGHT ME

by ELVIS A. PRESLEY

5. *BLANK BOOK* ELVIS HAD MADE UP TO AMUSE FRIENDS. RECENTLY AUCTIONED BY SOTHEBY'S.

(LEVI & CAT ARE IN HELL)

IX. WILDS, WOODS, & GAS

LAST SUNDAY

MONDAY

TUESDAY

WEDNESDAY

THURSDAY

X. I GOT A MILLION OF 'EM

Artist's representation of a patient's phantom limb, which has the perplexing feeling of penetrating the solid mattress, with foot resting on the floor.

XI. HELL

CONTINUED...

XII. ESCAPE

COLOUR ILLUSTRATION FROM 'SURREALIST GAMES' (REDSTONE PRESS, LONDON)

XIII. TELL ME A STORY

LEVIATHAN
by PETER BLEGVAD

PART IV ~ Synopsis:
CAT IS TELLING *LEVI* A STORY IN WHICH A *FATHER* SELLS HIS *SON* TO THE *DEVIL*. A *WOLF* CARRIES THE *SON* TO WHERE *THREE MAIDENS* ARE *BATHING*.

WAIT! DON'T *TELL* ME - LET ME *GUESS*. THE *SON* STEALS THE *CLOTHES* OF THE *YOUNGEST MAIDEN* WHO TURNS OUT TO BE THE *DEVIL'S DAUGHTER*, & SHE HELPS HIM OUTWIT HER *FATHER* & THEY LIVE *HAPPILY EVER AFTER*.

THEY COME TO WHERE *THREE MAIDENS* ARE *BATHING*.

NOW YOU MUST STEAL THE CLOTHES OF WHEN SHE COMES OUT SHE'LL SAY: HAS MY CLOTHES?' I'LL GET WHOEVER TROUBLE HE'S IN, IF HE'LL ONLY G

YOUNGEST MAIDEN. CLOTHES?' WHO THEM OUT OF ANY THEM *BACK*!'

YOU'VE HEARD IT BEFORE!

IN *SEVERAL* VARIANTS, THE *FATHERS* ALWAYS GET THE *WORST* OF IT. THE POOR *DEVIL* IS *BETRAYED* BY THE *DAUGHTER* HE LOVED & TRUSTED. BUT IT'S THE *HERO'S* FATHER I FEEL *SORRIEST* FOR.

BUT HE *SOLD* HIS SON TO THE *DEVIL*!

I *KNOW*. IN RETURN FOR A FOOLPROOF WAY TO CHEAT HIS CRONIES AT *GAMBLING*...

RIGHT! HE WINS A *FORTUNE!* THAT'S HIS *VILLA!*

BUT I DON'T THINK HE'S IN ANY *FRAME OF MIND* TO *ENJOY* HIS *RICHES!* THINK OF HIS *REMORSE!* IMAGINE THE *ABHORENCE* HIS *WIFE* & *DAUGHTER* WOULD FEEL FOR HIM! HAVING *RUINED* HIS FORMER *CRONIES*, HE'D BE LEFT *ALONE* WITH HIS HORRID *FLY* - NO DOUBT SEEKING *JUSTIFICATION* FOR HIS *SELFISHNESS* BY BLAMING HIS *OWN* FATHER'S INDIFFERENCE TO HIM, & HIS *FATHER'S FATHER'S* INDIFFERENCE, & *SO ON*, BACK TO *ADAM* - A LEGACY OF *MORAL FAILURE* WHICH ULTIMATELY *POINTS THE FINGER* AT A CALLOUS, JEALOUS, SMALL-MINDED *GOD*. THE *MORAL* OF THE TALE IS CLEAR; FROM *HENCEFORTH*, WHENEVER I HEAR THE *BUZZING* OF A *FLY*, I'LL BE *STEELED* IN MY *RESOLVE* TO *NEVER* HAVE *CHILDREN*.

DO YOU KNOW THE ONE ABOUT THE *THREE BEARS*?

The End

HELP ME! PLEEZE!

LEVIATHAN
by Peter Blegvad

SNIFF TELL ME A STORY!

THEN YOU PROMISE TO STOP CRYING & GO TO SLEEP?

I PROMISE. MAKE IT A *TRUE* STORY LIKE LAST TIME, BUT WITH A *CHILD PROTAGONIST*. PLEEZE?

O.K. THEN. ONCE UPON A TIME, "WHEN LITTLE *ARPAD* WAS 2½ YEARS OLD, HE TRIED, WHILE AT A SUMMER RESORT, TO *URINATE INTO THE CHICKEN COOP*, ...

...& ON THIS OCCASION A CHICKEN *BIT HIS PENIS* OR PECKED AT IT. WHEN HE RETURNED TO THE SAME PLACE A YEAR LATER HE *BECAME A CHICKEN HIMSELF*, ...

...WAS INTERESTED *ONLY* IN THE CHICKEN COOP & GAVE UP HUMAN SPEECH FOR *CACKLING* & *CROWING*. DURING THE PERIOD OF OBSERVATION, AT THE AGE OF 5, HE SPOKE AGAIN, ...

LITTLE ARPAD'S "MIND'S EYE"

...BUT HIS SPEECH WAS EXCLUSIVELY ABOUT CHICKENS & OTHER FOWL. HE PLAYED WITH NO OTHER TOY ...

I'M NOT A TOY. A CHICKEN IS FOR LIFE!

...& SANG ONLY SONGS IN WHICH THERE WAS SOMETHING ABOUT *POULTRY*."

ZZZZ

TEXT FROM: "THE INFANTILE RECURRENCE OF TOTEMISM" by SIGMUND FREUD

XIV. SONGS

fig A.

"DO YOU FEAR THE FORCE OF THE WIND?" by HAMLIN GARLAND

XVI. A PROBLEM AIRED

MAP OF THE 'HOOD (CHILDHOOD)

LEVI & CAT VISIT SITES IN THE 'HOOD.
THIS WEEK: *REMEMBRANDT'S* STUDIO.

I'M ENJOYING YOUR VISIT
SO MUCH!
I CAN'T WAIT FOR IT TO
BE *OVER* SO I CAN
REMEMBER IT!

EXTERIOR

I LOOK *FORWARD*
TO LOOKING *BACK.*

LIKE *HER* ?

LOT'S WIFE. YES, HERS WAS THE
ULTIMATE IN *RETROSPECTIVE*
FERVOUR. THIS *RELIQUARY*
HOLDS HER REMAINS.

HER *ASHES,*
PERHAPS?

S

NOT EXACTLY ...

LEVIATHAN by PETER BLEGVAD

SOME PEOPLE CAN'T STAND TO HEAR THEMSELVES ON TAPE.

SOME CAN'T BEAR TO SEE THEM- SELVES ON FILM.

LEVI CAN'T STAND THE SIGHT OF HIS OWN VOICE IN PRINT.

LEVIATHAN
by Peter Blegvad

Q: WHAT DEFINES "CHARACTER"?

A: THE CHOICES A PERSON MAKES UNDER PRESSURE.

THE CHARACTER - LEVI

THE PRESSURE - EQUIVALENT TO 500 ATMOSPHERES

THE CHOICES

Q: WHICH DO YOU PREFER?

TWO PEAS IN A POD! BUT THEY'RE SO ALIKE!

Q: WHICH WOULD YOU SAVE FROM A BURNING BUILDING?

a.

b.

CHALK & CHEESE! BUT THEY'RE SO DIFFERENT!

WITH HIS OXYGEN RUNNING OUT, KNOWING HIS DECISIONS, ONCE MADE, WILL BE IRREVOCABLE, LEVI INVOKES A HIGHER POWER TO ENLIGHTEN HIS JUDGEMENT.

EENIE MEENIE MINIE MO...

LEVIATHAN

by PETER BLEGVAD

ERWIN SCHRÖDINGER, NOBEL-PRIZEWINNING PHYSICIST, PROPOSES AN *EXPERIMENT* TO ILLUSTRATE THE *PECULIAR* THEORY THAT AN *ATOM* CAN OCCUPY *2 STATES* AT THE *SAME TIME!* (ALTHOUGH ANY ATTEMPT TO *OBSERVE* IT WILL FORCE THE ATOM TO ADOPT *ONE* STATE OR THE *OTHER!*)

(AHEM!) *LADIES & GENTLEMEN!* I PROPOSE THAT WE SHUT AN *IMAGINARY CAT* IN A BOX WITH A *CANNISTER* OF *CYANIDE* TRIGGERED TO *OPEN* BY THE *DECAY* OF A *RADIOACTIVE ATOM.*

HE'S BEHIND THIS STONE.

!

QUANTUM THEORY SAYS THAT, UNTIL THE ATOM'S STATE IS *OBSERVED*, IT EXISTS IN A *SUPERPOSITION* OF ITS *UNDECAYED & DECAYED* STATES. BUT, THIS SUPPOSES THAT THE *CAT* MUST *ALSO* BE IN A SUPERPOSITION, i.e. SIMULTANEOUSLY *ALIVE & DEAD.*

CONNECTICUT

STATE LINE

NEW JERSEY

HELLO, *R.S.P.C.I.A.?* I WISH TO REPORT AN *UNETHICAL EXPERIMENT.*

I USE THIS *PARADOX* TO ILLUSTRATE THE *DIFFICULTY* OF CONNECTING QUANTUM MECHANICS...

AHH, *GOOD!* I *THOUGHT* SO, BUT I WANTED TO BE *SURE.* THANK YOU! GOOD BYE.

... WITH THE LAWS OF *CLASSICAL PHYS...* * HEY! GET *BACK! NO!* NICE KITTY... *HELP! AUGGGHHHH...*

SHOULDN'T WE LEND A *HAND?*

THE *R.S.P.C.I.A.* ASSURED ME THERE'S NO NEED...

* TEXT ADAPTED FROM MARK WARD'S ARTICLE IN *NEW SCIENTIST,* JUNE 1, 1996

I PUT THE *BOFFIN* IN HIS *COFFIN!*

THE CAT IN THE HAT

THE *REAL* IS NO MATCH FOR THE *IMAGINARY.*

R e S P e C t Imaginary Animals!

XVII. THE TRUCK IS STUCK